CW00864373

MIRACLES
ALLOTTED TO CHRIS

MIRACLES ALLOTTED TO CHRIS

CHRISTOPHER DUMAIS

COPYRIGHT © 2020 BY CHRISTOPHER DUMAIS.

ISBN:	HARDCOVER	978-1-7960-9010-9
	SOFTCOVER	978-1-7960-9011-6
	EBOOK	978-1-7960-9014-7

All rights reserved. No part of this book may be reproduced or transmitted in any form or by any means, electronic or mechanical, including photocopying, recording, or by any information storage and retrieval system, without permission in writing from the copyright owner.

Scripture quotations marked NKJV are taken from the New King James Version. Copyright © 1982 by Thomas Nelson, Inc. Used by permission. All rights reserved.

Scripture quotations marked KJV are from the Holy Bible, King James Version (Authorized Version). First published in 1611. Quoted from the KJV Classic Reference Bible, Copyright © 1983 by The Zondervan Corporation.

Any people depicted in stock imagery provided by Getty Images are models, and such images are being used for illustrative purposes only.
Certain stock imagery © Getty Images.

Print information available on the last page.

Rev. date: 02/24/2020

To order additional copies of this book, contact:
Xlibris
1-888-795-4274
www.Xlibris.com
Orders@Xlibris.com
808512

CONTENTS

MY FIRST WELDING JOB

The first miracle I could remember was when I was in high school in the tenth grade. I took a class that was a combination of wood and metal shop. Both wood and metal creations would be required for us to receive a passing grade. I found out right away that I gravitated toward metals much more than wood, so I learned as much about welding as that class could teach me. I was looking forward to next year when I could take metal shop and really start learning about what would become my forty-year career in the metals trade.

When it was time to elect classes for eleventh grade, my eyes searched the page to find the place that said "metal shop," and I eagerly checked that box. But much to my surprise, the teacher saw talent in me where welding was concerned and started calling me over when he saw me enter the classroom. He showed me how to use a TIG welder, and it seemed like, every day, he would ask me to weld special projects for his friends or coworkers. By the end of that year, my teacher received a call from a man who needed a high school student to operate an MIG welder for the manufacture of off-road truck products. So thanks to my teacher and a welding test, I had my first welding job.

After about a year and a half at that job, I was falsely accused of ripping off Cokes from their vending machine and was fired. So not knowing what to do next, I started on the five-mile walk back to my mom's house, where I lived. As I made my way down the street, I noticed, just two buildings away, a company that manufactured motorcycle wheels for street bikes. So I walked into the office and asked if they were hiring welders. The man asked me if I could use a TIG welder, and I said, "Yes, sir!" (not really having enough TIG experience to do the work). So he invited me into the welding shop and gave me a TIG weld test. That was where the miracle manifested itself. I sat down on the welding bench and laid down a weld so perfect I couldn't believe my eyes. The next thing I knew, he was asking me when I could start. I said, "Today," and he made a spot for me that night on the third shift.

That night, I not only learned my new job but I also noticed I could weld as good as some of the professional ex-aerospace welders who worked there. After a month or so, my boss said they had to close the third shift and asked me to come to the second shift, which I did. About two months later, they shut down the second shift and asked me if I could come to the first shift, so I did. (I had to drop out of high school for that shift, but I went at night to get my diploma.) Then finally, the company closed, and I was out searching for my next adventure.

THE SHROUD OF TURIN

The first miracle God used to get my attention occurred in 1983, when I was twenty-three years of age. At the time, I was living and working in the San Fernando Valley in Los Angeles County. Most weekends, I'd make the three-hour drive down to San Diego County to my mom's house in Santee to visit my family. And on that Sunday night, like most Sunday nights at her house, I asked her to wake me up at 3:00 a.m. so I could beat the Monday morning traffic through Los Angeles. So I kissed her goodbye and drove away at 3:30 a.m.

I remembered it was a clear night without a moon, so I decided that when I got on I-5 north, I would turn off my headlights through Camp Pendleton Marine Base and set my cruise control to ninety-five miles per hour so I could make it in good time. As I was sitting there, patting myself on the back for coming up with such a great idea, I fell asleep at the wheel.

Suddenly, I was awakened by a voice above me saying,

"Wake up, son!" As I opened my eyes, I realized my Chevy Z28 was going under the trailer of an 18-wheeler. Before I could cover my face with my hands, I felt the car slow down without me pushing on the brake pedal, then the voice spoke to me again, saying, "Take control of your vehicle, son!" Immediately, I threw my hands on the steering wheel and my foot on the brake pedal. As I got the car under (my) control and the distance between the trailer and my car increased, I noticed the whole back of the trailer was turning into the face on the Shroud of Turin. I literally panicked and floored my accelerator as I took off around the 18-wheeler. I was shaking all over as I drove away, but I couldn't believe what had happened. So I slowed down to get behind the trailer again, and as I drove behind it, all that I saw was the roll-up door, no face. So as I proceeded to change lanes, I took one more look up at the door when suddenly, Jesus' face appeared again, scaring me almost to death.

Understandably, I think back to that event now and then and thank the Lord Jesus Christ for saving me on that moonless morning.

THE WONDER OF TONGUES

One day, I was over at my cousin's house for a barbecue.

While we were finishing our meals, I suddenly started crying and speaking in an unknown language. As I wiped my eyes and apologized, my cousin said, "Dude, that was beautiful!" As I watched him drying his eyes, he explained that I just spoke in tongues. So I asked him what that was, and while he was telling me, his wife asked what I had said, so he gave her the interpretation, saying, "Chris said it's breaking his heart to see your sister and her husband getting divorced!" So he asked me if that was right, and I said yes, so he gave me a briefing on biblical tongues as we finished up our dinners. To this day, I haven't spoken in tongues at all since that night.

That was three years before I was born again, and people would say to me that I couldn't have spoken in tongues before

I was born again. So I would tell them that if God spoke to Balaam through a donkey and Jesus said that rocks would cry out if He stopped the people from crying out, then He could cause me to speak in tongues before I was born again.

DON'T TOUCH MY CHOSEN

At another barbecue at my cousin's house (it was a graduation party for fifty new police officers, of whom my cousin was one), I was sitting there feeling no pain, thanks to the pain meds I was taking due to a surgery on my left knee just the day before. As I watched the festivities, my cousin suggested that the men should play a game called chicken, where two men stand side to side and try to throw each other to the ground. The man still standing wins.

Watching my cousin as he threw forty-nine officers to the ground, I was speechless. All of a sudden, he looked at me and said, "Ok Chris, you're next!" So I started laughing and said back to him, "That's a good one, bro!"

But then he got this strange look on his face and said, "Don't make me come and get you!"

So I started protesting, pointing out that the police are supposed to serve and protect their communities, not throw people in casts or crutches to the ground, but it made no difference. He wouldn't listen, so I grabbed my crutches and made my way to where he was standing. When I was next to him, he said, "Get your arm up here." So as I did, I closed my eyes 'cause I didn't want to see the ground coming at me. I remembered hearing "One, two, three," and as I waited to hit the ground, nothing happened. So I opened my eyes, expecting him to say, "Got you!" But much to my surprise, he was flying across the front yard.

As he flipped over, landing hard on his back, I thought to myself, *I'm a dead man!* So as I watched him get to his feet charging at me, I yelled, "Knock it off!" But that had no effect. He just demanded I get my arm up again. So as I assumed the position and closed my eyes, again I heard "One, two, three." Opening my eyes, I stood shocked as I watched him repeating the same flight path as before, but this time, when he hit the ground, he couldn't get up. As at least one hundred people watched him struggle to get on his feet, he spun around to look at me, and when I saw his face, I saw fear like I've never seen on his face before or since. Then he walked to the unlit street where we all watched him light a cigarette.

So before I could make sense of all that, I heard a voice from behind me, saying, "So, you think you're tough, do you?" And

I spun around to see a man who was trained in the martial arts grab me by the right arm and proceed to throw me over his head. So there I was over this guy's head, crutches and all, heading for the ground when suddenly, he and I traded places. So as I landed on my good foot and crutches, what seemed to be my turn hitting the ground turned out to be him hitting the ground. Now I was really pissed when I heard my cousin coming from the street yelling the man's name and threatening to put him in jail if he didn't stop his attack.

So what can I say, this all happened in front of over one hundred witnesses, and the beauty of this story was when my brother (who understandably wouldn't believe this story) asked our cousin if it was true, my cousin said, "Yep!"

A DECISION MADE

About three years later, I found myself a drug addict and mad that my leg was never going to be the same again, keeping me from doing the things I loved to do. I started having thoughts about taking my own life, but at that time, strange things started happening.

One day, I went out, and when I returned home, I noticed three Bibles on the dinning room table where I would sit and do drugs. So scratching my head, I began to read these three Bibles, not knowing how or why they got there. Many hours of reading passed and becoming tired, I went to my room to go to bed. As I started disrobing, I reached over and took my .357 from its holster and raised it to my head, squeezing the trigger. I started crying saying to the Lord, "Please, Jesus, don't let me die and go to hell!" The next thing I knew, it was morning, and realizing I wasn't dead, I became angry because I knew I would have to endure another day of self-destruction.

So arriving again at the end of the next day, I retired to my room to get some sleep, and after disrobing, I took my gun once again to my head. Repeating the same prayer, I said, "Please, Jesus, don't let me die and go to hell!" So just like the day before, I woke up alive again, this time more mad than before. That exact same scene happened three more nights till I woke up alive again on Saturday morning. Sitting on the edge of my bed, I realized God heard my prayers all five times. It just took me five times to get it. So looking out my bedroom window, I excitedly asked, "Lord, what are we going to do today?"

So I decided to go visit my aunt, and when I arrived at her house, something strange happened. Instead of getting out of my truck, I drove away to a park close to her house and stopped my truck, not knowing why. As I watched people enjoying birthday parties with their kids, I noticed the blue sky becoming very dark and the wind starting to blow really hard. As I watched the panicking people trying to load their families into their cars before what looked like rain at any moment, I started feeling something I never felt before, a strange feeling.

As the last car drove away, I became very peaceful, then as I watched the clouds swirling above me, I noticed a red car pull into the parking lot and park next to me. As I looked over, I saw a man shaking and getting out of my truck I said to him, "Hey, get out of your car. God is here!" So as the man got out and walked to be next to me, I suddenly put my left hand on his right shoulder and, lifting my right hand and pointing at the clouds, I said, "Behold He cometh with clouds and every eye shall see Him, and those who also pierced Him" (Rev. 1:7). Then I heard Jesus say to me, "Come and sit on this park bench!" So I said to the man, "Come on. God wants us to go and sit on that bench." But then the man said to me, "But He wants me to leave!" So I said, "Then obey and do what He tells you to do!" And with that, the man said to me, "I am now a warrior for the Lord Jesus Christ!" And he returned to his car and drove away, never to be seen by me again.

So as I started walking toward the park bench the Lord showed me, I was suddenly stopped by Jesus, saying, "You are not worthy of Me if you don't forsake this world for My sake!" So He explained that He wanted me to return to my truck and empty my pockets, then take the little Bible that was on the dashboard (which was given to me that morning) and return to the park bench and sit down. After I sat down, all my motor skills were taken from me, and so was my vision. As I sat there quite nervous, the Lord Jesus, using my hands, opened the little Bible I was holding, and tilting my head down, He returned my vision as I read, "I am the Alpha and the Omega, the First and the Last, the Beginning and End" (Rev. 22:13).

As you could imagine, I was shook up but excited to think that just twelve hours ago, I was trying to take my life, and now I was being instructed by the Author of life. Then He took me to Psalm 103:12, and I heard Him say, "Now, son, I'm washing your sins." Then He finished the sentence with the written word of Psalm 103:12 while I read: "As far as the east is from the west, so far hath He removed our transgressions from us."

While I was reading, water suddenly fell from above me and washed over me twice, soaking the Bible and me. After that, the Lord Jesus formed a curtain of water around me as if to protect me, and it flowed for the next nine hours till He released me at 3:00 a.m. Now I'm off-the-charts excited, wondering what's next. (If you're wondering, I still have that Bible, and yes, the pages are all swollen and much thicker than when it was new. Please see the photo on the cover page.) So following my "what's next" question, my head returned to the forward-looking position, and as I looked into what seemed to be a thick fog, I started to see something approaching me. Not able to move my head or hands (which is normal for a person to do when something is heading to their face), I started to see what looked like a dove hovering in front of me. Unable to blink my eyes from the wind coming from His see-through wings and onto my dripping face, I said to Him in my mind, *I know who you are. You're the Holy Spirit of God!* And with that, He flew into my face. (OK, at that point, I thought I needed to stop asking what's next.)

After that, the Lord Jesus took me on a tour of His Word, the Bible, and showed me many things, one of which would be a new name He had given to me that He allowed me to watch as He typed it on one of the blank pages (as if from an invisible typewriter) at the back of the Bible that was now in the Lamb's Book of Life. It was very long, and I couldn't pronounce it. Then He showed me a moving picture of our Statue of Liberty shown from the left side of my head while I was reading the Bible, which was still in front of me, turned to Revelations 17 and 18. (It was as if He made my left ear into an eye.) There the Lord Jesus showed me the destruction of the USA, and when I was reading Revelation 18, I saw explosions going off behind the Statue of Liberty. A very sobering thing indeed!

Throughout the night, Jesus called me son, and I got this weird idea that I was something more than I really was. So as my head started to think pridefully, I started to feel a very cold wind inside the water curtain. I realized that the Lord was correcting my thinking. As I struggled to find heat from my body, my eyes returned to the Bible, and I started to read Psalm 27:1–3, "The Lord is my light and my salvation," etc. But suddenly, I realized that I couldn't read any further because my thumbs had rubbed off the words due to me squeezing the pages because of the cold wind I was experiencing. So I became scared, and as I struggled to find a solution, the Lord Jesus Christ removed the water curtain and returned my vision and motor skills. As I came to my senses, I realized that I felt half-frozen, and trying to move and spin around to see my truck, I began the long struggle to get back to it. (This is where the fear of the Lord began for me.)

As I said above, the Lord released me at 3:00 a.m., and I made my way back to my truck and fell into a fitful sleep. This was around the date April 15, 1986.

THE SHAKING

One day, I was at a friend's house where I was talking about the things of God. My friends were in the garage getting their dirt bikes ready for a trip to the desert. I stayed up all night with them, preaching what was the limited Word of God that I knew at that time.

At about 5:00 a.m., one of the guys who was renting the house became very angry at me and started to raise his voice and yell at me. I did my best to answer his questions, but he only became madder. So the next thing I knew, all three of them were in my face, and the man renting the home suddenly stuck his face about an inch from mine and yelled, "If God told you to preach to us, you better show us a miracle now!"

So looking down at my little Bible (the one I had in the park) I started to pray asking the Lord to not let the beating I was about to receive hurt too bad. Then the Lord Jesus Christ lifted my head, and opening my mouth, said to the man with the demands, "What would you boys like, an earthquake?" With the Lord's question asked, the county of San Diego started to shake violently. It was between a magnitude 4.6 and 5.2 earthquake. As I watched the three men run out of the garage, hitting their heads on the half-closed door and stopping in the middle of the street, I heard the Lord say to me, "Go in the house and tell the dog to get off the couch, then rest!" And with that, I went in to find a large Irish setter and said, "Get down, boy." And after he did, I took his place for an hour before I said goodbye and drove away. Peace!

REBUKE, DON'T SHOOT

One night, I was on my bed reading the Bible when I heard the dogs barking. So I got up to see what the problem was, and as I looked at the dogs, I noticed they were looking at something. When I saw what they saw, I took off running. It was a green spirit of some kind coming out of a boulder, and it was already about twelve feet tall by the time I was running. So in a panic, I cried out "Give me back my gun!" to my brother as I tried to break down his bedroom door (I had given the gun to him because I was told by the Lord that I couldn't trust Him and Smith & Wesson). Then suddenly the Lord said, "You can't stop a demon with a material weapon. You must use My Word!" So I stopped banging on my brother's door and ran to the back sliding door. Opening the door (only an inch), I yelled, "I rebuke you, Satan, in the name of the Lord Jesus Christ!" Then I slammed the door. And much to my surprise, the demon stopped ascending, but it was still there. So I nervously opened the door again and repeated the same command I used before, and the demon started descending until it disappeared.

So sitting down in the chair next to me, I watched the seven dogs run up to the boulder and start digging. Then my brother came running out of his room with a rifle and asked me what was going on. So I told him what I just went through, then he said, "Come on!" So I said, "You don't have to believe me, but you better believe those seven witnesses that are tearing their nails off on that boulder in your backyard!" And as he turned to look, he saw the dogs still digging like crazy. I moved to Los Angeles shortly after that event, but my brother could no longer deny the events he had witnessed in my life, and he gave his life to Christ too.

A LETTER INTERCEPTED

One night, I was reading the Bible on my bed (still renting a room from my brother) when I heard the voice of the Lord say to me, "Go get the mail!" So I jumped in my truck and drove down the 1,100-foot-long driveway. After retrieving the three envelopes, I started driving back to the house. As I was checking to see if there was something for me, I noticed one letter that didn't have a return address. I thought that the handwriting looked a lot like my mom's or my dad's, and as I pondered that thought, I heard the Lord say, "When you get to the house, open that letter, read the contents, then destroy it by fire!" So when I got to the kitchen, I read the letter God showed me, and I began to cry. It was a letter from my dad to my brother with an attorney's letterhead inside that my dad and oldest sister had signed with one blank line with my brother's name typed and a place for him to sign. It was a letter that would need three signatures in order to have me committed. So as I did what the

Lord commanded me, holding the burning letter over the sink, Jesus said to me, "Woe to those who try to hurt my chosen ones. Nothing shall happen to them unless I allow it!" After that, I retired to my room and fell sleep.

NO SMOKING

One day, my friend and I were at my mom's house swimming. When we got out of the pool, we sat down, and both of us lit a cigarette. As we were puffing away, the Lord said to me, "Thou shall not pollute the temple of the Lord any longer!"

So I looked at my friend and asked, "What did you say?"

He looked at me and said, "I didn't say anything!"

So I took another puff, and suddenly, I heard the Lord repeat the same command. So I looked at my friend and asked him again, "What did you say?" And he said, "Nothing!"

So at that point, I became very nervous because I liked smoking four packs a day. So I silently asked, "Was that you, Lord?" So after not hearing anything else, I took another puff, and I almost couldn't keep myself from vomiting. The smell and taste were so bad that I ran into the house to find my new carton, and opening a pack, I took the first puff and had to lean over the sink to be sick. After washing my face, I went to the backyard and put the carton down and told my friend, "God just removed this habit from me, just like He did with the cocaine and crystal methamphetamine. This house is clean!"

TRAMPLE ON SCORPIONS

One night, I was on my bed reading the Bible when I decided to go to the kitchen to get a beverage. As I turned the corner and flipped on the light, I heard a crunching sound under my foot. When I looked down, I saw a scorpion with his left claw smashed and stuck to the floor and his green blood running out. So I instinctively jumped back and watched this guy trying to sting something. As I watched (from a safe distance), the Lord suddenly said to me, "Pick it up and kill it in the garbage disposal!" So there I was, trying to figure out how to do that without getting stung. So I finally got this great idea that if I fold a paper towel four times, I should be able to grab it without getting stung. So there I went, grabbing the tail from behind and rushing it over to the garbage disposal where I made the deposit. Feeling proud of myself after reading where Jesus said we could trample on scorpions, Luke 10:9, I returned to my room to continue reading the Bible.

But twenty years later, the Lord showed me that I disobeyed His Word when I used the paper towel instead of my bare hand to pick up the scorpion. He showed me in Numbers 20:11 where Moses struck the rock twice instead of speaking to it to command the water to come forth. I hoped I've learned my lesson on that test.

MY LEG HEALED

One morning, I was awakened by the phone. So flying out of bed, I raced down the hallway, made the ninety-degree turn toward the kitchen, and picked up the phone just before my mom hung up, saying, "Good morning, Mom, what's new?"

She asked me, "Why are you breathing so hard, son?"

So I thought for a moment, then said, "God healed my leg. That's the first time I've ran in three years!"

So she said, "Aw, come on, son, don't make up stories."

So rather than argue, I told her I would come over and show her. When I arrived at her house, I gave her a complete demonstration, and she couldn't believe it. I barely could.

I explained to her that the Lord told me while I was praying that if I let Him have the vengeance on the doctor who mistreated me (Psalm 94), he would heal my leg, but if I sued the doctor, I would win the $250,000 lawsuit. So I got off my knees, and finding the lawsuit, I got a good grip and ripped it to pieces and threw it in the trash and said, "Lord, I want my leg back!" When I woke up the next morning, my leg was healed. So she just stared in amazement, and I was so thankful to Jesus for this healing.

THE GRIM REAPER

One night, my dad asked me if I wanted to go to dinner with him and my little sister, so I said yes, and he picked me up. When we arrived at the restaurant, my sister and dad became very scared about something, but I didn't know what. So as my dad parked the car and we got out, I noticed a figure standing in the dark part of the parking lot in front of a closed-down doughnut shop. Then my dad suddenly grabbed my sister and me around the neck and started for the restaurant. So taking his arm off my neck, I made my way over to this fellow to see if I could help him in any way. When I approached him, I could see he was wearing a full-length cloak with a hood over his head. As I started telling him about Jesus, I noticed there wasn't anybody in the cloak. I looked for hands, but there weren't any. I looked for feet or shoes, but there weren't any. I looked for a face, but there wasn't one. Suddenly, I knew why my dad and sister were scared. It was the Grim Reaper but without his sickle. So

I excused myself, and doing one of the fastest U-turns on the planet, I made my way back to the restaurant where I found my dad and little sister doing their best to recover. Me? I just counted my blessings and kept my mouth shut.

THIS LITTLE INDIAN

One afternoon, I was at a launder mat washing my clothes when all of a sudden, I could hear what sounded like seven different sirens. As I exited the building, I could see a red car race into the intersection with four sheriff cars following, sirens and lights blasting. All of a sudden, there was a loud crash, and as the red car came to a stop after T-boning another car, I saw a man with hair down to his pants jump out and start running toward me through the parking lot. With the sheriffs in hot pursuit, I watched to see what this guy would do. I started praying and thanking Jesus for healing my leg and asked him to let me catch this guy before he hurts somebody or tries to take a child hostage, reminding Him I didn't make it to the LAPD back before He healed my leg.

Next thing I knew, I'm running right toward the guy watching and zigzagging, matching his every move. Suddenly, the man and I collided head-on, and as I wrapped my arms around him and squeezed with all my might, the man said, "Please don't kill me!" So I told him I wasn't going to kill him, but I was going to hand him over to the sheriff. At that point was when one of the sheriff cars skidded right next to me, and as the officer approached, I handed the man over to him and went back to finish my laundry. Just another day in the life of this Christian.

BE STILL

Another time, a friend of mine asked if I could give him a ride to Lakeside so he could meet with a friend, so we jumped in my truck and took off. When we arrived, I beheld an amazing ranch for horses, so we got out and walked to the front of the truck and started looking around for Jose's friend when all of a sudden, this huge Doberman pinscher came flying through the screen door at the main house, coming right toward us, fangs and all. So Jose and I did what every unarmed human would do—we turned around and started running. As we passed the safety of my F-150, I realized we were now in the middle of a training arena for the horses, and there was no way we could outrun this dog. So I thought, *I just have to outrun Jose, right?* (New leg, don't fail me now!) Right when I thought I had a good plan, both of us came to an abrupt stop, and with our bodies spinning around, we realized God had just changed our plans.

Now we were walking right toward this charging dog, and neither one of us could get free from God's grip.

So all I could do was go along for the ride knowing how afraid of dogs I was when suddenly, this dog locked on to me and, what seemed to be one hundred miles per hour, stuffed his nose right into my private parts. (The amazing part of this was when the dog hit me, there wasn't any forward inertia that should have knocked me down). Then if that was not enough, the Lord had the dog lift up his nose while he was still buried in my junk. So as I found myself at that point standing on tiptoes and starting to shake like the cowardly lion as he stood in front of the Wizard of Oz, I began to plead with the Lord, asking, "Please, Lord, remove this dog from me and make him lie down so I can get to the safety of my truck." So much to my surprise, the dog walked away and lay down. So there I was, shaking like a leaf finally sitting in my truck as I watched Jose find his friend and hug him. So I drove away (done for that day) and headed home, realizing how close I got to becoming a eunuch.

But about twenty years later, I started doubting many of those miracles, so the Lord sent Jose back into my life only for a moment at a 7-Eleven store in El Cajon. And when I saw him, I asked if the event at the horse ranch with the dog really happened or if it was a dream. Jose said to me, "Yes, senor, it really happened. Never forget what the Lord did for us that day!" So I'll take Jose's advice and trust in the Lord with all my heart, and lean not on my own understanding (Proverbs 3:5). I wish everybody could.

BOAT TRAILER HEADACHE

One morning at work, I had to modify a boat trailer for a customer. While I was setting up the cutting torch and welder, I started feeling uncomfortable. I asked the Lord what was wrong when suddenly, I saw a vision appear in front of me of a clamp. As I watched the vision disappear, I wondered what the Lord was trying to tell me, but I kept on working, still uneasy. And as I pressed the oxygen trigger and started cutting the metal frame, I heard a bang, and then the lights went out. The next thing I heard was Jesus saying, "Sit up, son, and turn off the torch!"

As I opened my eyes and sat up (but not under my own power, I believe an angel lifted me up), I struggled to see through the blood that was flowing from my head onto my face. I finally found the cutting torch and turned the valve to the off position, then I fell back onto the parking lot. My boss rushed me to the hospital where I received stitches and x-rays, and after a week off work, I returned to my job. Later that week, I told my boss that if the Lord wouldn't have told me to turn off the torch, I would have been burned really bad. He confirmed that thought by telling me that when he started to finish that job, as soon as he lit the cutting torch, the feed lines blew up. It was because when the trailer hit me in the head, I dropped the torch, and the flame was burning the feed lines. That was a close call.

So I came to the conclusion that the Lord was trying to tell me to secure the boat trailer with clamps because the weight of the boat on the trailer would be too much, and it would collapse on me. He was right again.

THE SAMSON ARM

One day when I returned home from work, I walked into my apartment, and I was hit head-on by a blast of heat. It was because the wall-mounted air conditioner hadn't been fixed right for the tenth time, and being a welder, in the summer, I required a good air-conditioning unit. So I got really mad and yelled, "Lord, how can I put a ceiling fan in without touching the ceiling?" Suddenly, I saw a bright flash of light, and in this bright cloud, I saw a metal arm mounted in the corner of the room, holding a ceiling fan. So I ran over to my pen and paper and drew it before I forgot what it looked like.

The next day at work, I asked my boss if I could stay after so I could fabricate and weld this new idea. So two days later, I took it home and mounted it in the corner, then drove to the store to purchase a ceiling fan. After the fan was hanging from the new arm that I named the *Samson arm*, I sat back in my chair and marveled at this great idea the Lord came up with. I

41

chose to call it the Samson arm because of its strength, like the biblical character Samson. My pastor said that I should patent the Samson arm, so I did (see the photo on the cover). What a great idea!

WHY THE SUN

I remember a sister in the Lord who became sickened by a brain tumor. I didn't know her very well, but God put a burden on my heart to pray for her healing. So I decided to fast and pray. About three days later, I was driving home from work, and while I was praying for her, I noticed I was able to look right at the sun and drive at the same time without hurting my eyes. This went on for the four-mile stretch that took me west toward my apartment at sunset, when the sun hit you right in the eyes. I couldn't believe that it didn't hurt my eyes at all, so I wondered what God was up to. As I thought about my sister (who wasn't expected to survive this tumor), I returned home, and as I looked though my mail, I noticed a letter that was sent from her. Then I was filled with joy to read the good news that the tumor was in remission, and she was going to train to be a chaplain at the hospital by her house.

I knew that looking at the sun for that length of time was God's way of telling me that he heard our prayers and granted our petitions for our sister in Christ.

BEAT IT

I remembered when I bought my first boat, I was really sick with Rheumatoid Arthritis, and I just wanted to sit and relax while fishing. So I took the boat out to San Diego Bay and threw in a line to see what would happen. I started catching tons of fish (which didn't allow for much relaxation) and was almost unable to handle the work involved to land them all.

As I was enjoying myself, a game warden pulled up in his boat and asked to see my catch. So I excitedly raised my basketful of fish and watched as he looked through the basket. The next thing I knew, he pointed out two illegal sized white sea bass and asked me to follow him over to his dock. When we arrived, he took the white sea bass from the basket and started measuring them. As I watched scared of what might happen to me, I heard the warden yell "Hold still, you damn fish!" while he tried to get their measurements, (because the fish were kicking for their lives).

When he was done, he told me that he could confiscate my boat and gear and that it was my responsibility to know the fishing laws in that state. Then he told me he wasn't going to take my property, but I would have to appear in court and possibly do jail time. Then he wrote me a ticket with an order to appear. So before I pulled away, I asked the warden what he was going to do with the fish. He told me they would be frozen for evidence for the court. So I thanked him for going easy on me and pulled away from the dock.

Months later, I was driving down the freeway for my court appearance when I suddenly became emotional, and crying out to the Lord, I said, "I'm afraid, Lord. The warden said I could do jail time. What am I going to do?"

All of a sudden, the Lord spoke to me, saying, "When you get to court, ask your attorney why you're in trouble since the warden froze two perfectly healthy white sea bass."

So all of a sudden, I didn't feel afraid anymore, and I couldn't wait to get to the courthouse and meet my attorney. While I was sitting there, my attorney walked in, and we shook hands, then I immediately asked him what the Lord told me to, then he said to me, "Wait here!" As I watched him approach the bench and exchange words with the judge, I heard the judge say, "Get that man out of my courtroom!" And with that, my attorney walked toward me with a big smile and shook my hand and said, "You're done!" So I high tailed it out of there and went straight to the tackle shop to purchase all the fishing law books I could find. Keep on fishing!

DRY MY HANDS

One day, I was with my girlfriend, Carmen, and I was looking for some way to know if she was going to be my future wife. So as I watched her prepare dinner, I asked the Lord that if Carmen was going to be my wife someday, He would dry my sweaty palms as a sign, and I would take her hand and never let go. Suddenly, my hands became dryer than I had ever seen them, so I reached over and took her hand, while I was holding her hand, I thought to myself, *I can't hold her hand, I've got sweaty palms.* As soon as I thought that thought, my hands became sweaty once again, and panicking, I let go of her hand. As I realized that I just did what Peter did when he walked on the water to go to Jesus, and seeing the waves, he began to sink, I cried out, "Lord, forgive me. Please dry my hands again, and this time, I will hold both of her hands and never let go!" And immediately, my hands became dry again, and I reached over and took both her hands as she turned and smiled at me.

So that worked out good for both of us, and now we've been married for nineteen years, and many more!

LIFT UP YOUR LEG

Carmen's Story

On another day of fishing, my wife Carmen and I were out on our boat going for some more rainbow trout at Lake San Vicente. Those fish were hardy red meat rainbows averaging eighteen inches long. We were told by some men that all we had to do was go out to the buoy line and drop our night crawlers with no weights to about fifty feet, and we would catch our limits. Sure enough, we did catch our limits and decided that rather than go home early, we would stay and try to catch other kinds of fish. So we headed in to buy some ice and use the restroom.

As I waited in the boat for Carmen, I heard a noise that sounded like a body hitting the ground along with a bag of ice. So I spun around and saw Carmen lying facedown on the launch ramp. So I ran over to help her up when it became very apparent to me she would be needing the ice for her knee. After dropping the boat at home, I took her to the ER for x-rays where they told us she had a broken kneecap. They couldn't do surgery till the swelling went down, so Carmen lay in bed for a month.

Finally, the doctor said he couldn't delay the surgery any longer, so he scheduled Carmen for surgery. They had to shock her leg with electricity to relax the knee so they could put it in the proper position to do the surgery. Well, needless to say, they used too much current, causing Carmen's nerves to be non responsive keeping her from being able to walk for eleven months. And in those eleven months, her left leg atrophied down to nothing. But at that eleventh month marker, the Lord God came through with his faithfulness, and one day, while Carmen was lying in bed, she heard Him say, "Lift up your leg!" So she looked to see if I said it, but I was downstairs, so she waited to see if she would hear it again. And sure enough, she heard Him say again, "Lift up your leg!" So she struggled with all her might until her leg began to rise off the mattress. So she began the long struggle people go through to regain strength in their limbs as we rejoiced in the Lord, and to this day, it remains strong.

DOUGHNUTS TO EMPLOYMENT

I went back to a company ten years after they laid me off, and I was really nervous. You see, this was an aerospace company, and all the welds had to be x-rayed and checked with a die and black lights in completely dark rooms. Anyway, when I left the house to make my way to this company for my shakedown test, I decided to stop and get some doughnut holes in case I got hungry.

When I arrived, they gave me the different weld plates and three hours to complete them. So as I began to prep the welding surfaces, I started snacking on the doughnut holes, which was a mistake because I have type 2 diabetes, and when my blood sugar goes up, my vision gets bad. So as I started welding, I realized that I couldn't see anything, and I started to panic.

When I finished the first plate, one of the welders I used to work with came over to see how the weld looked. As he picked it up and looked it over, he said, "Dude, have you been practicing at home?"

So I said, "No, why?"

That was when he told me that he hadn't seen a weld that nice in a long time. So as he walked away, I wiped the sweat off my forehead and started welding the next plate. While I struggled to see (but couldn't), I asked God to forgive me for blowing my vision so bad that I probably wouldn't get the job.

When I finished, another welder whom I used to work with came over to check my work. Now this guy was the company's best welder. As he looked over the two plates, he mentioned to me, "Don't worry. You've got the job." So I thought to myself, *What's going on here? I can't even see how these welds looked while I was welding them, let alone after I was finished welding them.* But the guys kept on giving me a thumbs-up, so as I finished up the last two weld plates and cleaned up my mess, I realized that I was almost completely blind. (It took me more than the three hours given to the weld applicants to weld what normally would have taken me two hours.) Then the weld engineer who gave the tests to the applicants came and took the weld plates and the completed paperwork, then shook my hand and smiled and said, "You've got the job!" And after saying goodbye, I drove home barely able to see at all.

My conclusion? The only way those welds came out so good was the fact that Jesus, who also lives in this body with me, knew that He would have to step in and weld for me that day, the day that "doughnut blindness" tried to keep me from that job. Thank you, Lord Jesus!

V-BLADES

Back when I wasn't retired, I was a welder at an aerospace company in El Cajon, California. I worked on containment rings that were installed in jet engines for commercial airlines. These were manufactured out of aluminum extrusions that were rolled into rings, then welded together. The welds were x-rayed and sprayed with dye and examined under black lights to check for defects. I prided myself on being able to weld three and a half of the MIG-welded rings in an eight-hour shift.

I was having some back pain issues and had to stay out of work for two months. When I finally returned to work, I wasn't yet 100 percent better. I wasn't even 50 percent better, but I returned to work anyway. So I made my way over to the supervisor to ask him what he wanted me to do. He said V-blades, so grabbing my tools, I went to work. I paused to ask the Lord to just get me through these eight hours because my back was already hurting. At the end of the shift, I was doing my paperwork, and while I was counting how many parts I did, I noticed I had welded seven V-blades. As my heart started to race and sweat started to build up on my forehead, I cried out, "Lord, what have you done?" I knew I couldn't keep that pace every day. As a matter of fact, it was impossible to weld four V-blades in eight hours, or I would have done it by now. But seven? So God's ways being higher than our ways, I didn't have an answer as to what point God was making to me or somebody else that day other than this: that we can do all things through Christ Jesus who strengthens us (Phil. 4:13).

OLD MEN DREAM DREAMS

One night, when my wife was in Mexico City visiting her mom, I had a dream that I was at the Santee Lakes. When I arrived at the water's edge, I looked down and saw a small rainbow trout nibbling on some grass. I thought to myself, *That's weird, I didn't know trout ate grass.* The next thing I knew, it was already morning, so I decided to go fishing at the Santee Lakes just for some rest and recreation.

When I arrived, I got out of my truck and walked down to the water's edge to check it out. Saying to myself, *This looks like a great spot*, I went back to my truck to get my gear. After setting up and casting two lines, I sat back in my chair to wait for a bite. As I was looking around, I noticed this little rainbow trout at the water's edge chewing on a blade of grass. I couldn't believe my eyes. It was just like in the dream I had just five hours ago. So I caught it and put it on my stringer. About a half hour later, a man came up and asked if I had any luck. So I said, "I've got one!"

And as he looked down at it, he said, "Hey, you've caught a tagged fish!"

So I asked him what that was. He told me the little tag on the dorsal fin was worth a twenty-five-dollar gift card at Walmart. So I said, "Great!" and thanked him for telling me. Then he told me that they put really big rainbow trout in here, and the person who catches the biggest one would win a flat-screen TV. So I thanked him, and he drove away. So after six hours had passed, I started getting ready to go home when, suddenly, one of my lines took off. I battled for twenty minutes just to see the dorsal fin, and when I did, I knew I had a monster. That fish was the biggest rainbow trout I've ever caught. At twenty-eight inches, it was just one-fourth pound lighter than the fish a ten-year-old girl caught. She ended up winning the flat-screen TV. It was a good day at the office!

WHAT A WINDSHIELD

One day, I was reading the book of Psalms in my truck when I came across Psalm 27:10, where I read, "When your mother and father forsake you, I the Lord will take you up." Suddenly, I burst into tears and emptied my lungs. As I continued to empty my lungs I started to panic and I found myself unable to inhale. So right about the time I started to pass out, this strong wind came through my windshield and filled my lungs just in time for me to burst into a second round of tears. As the Lord walked me through that event, I finally became calm, and as I pondered what just happened, I realized that the Lord had started a healing process that would take thirty-four years and is still in the finishing-up stages even to this day. He made it clear to me that my parent's divorce did more damage to me than I would have ever thought possible.

It's sad to see the results of divorce in our modern times, but I guess it goes all the way back as far as prehistoric and recorded time. It is sad indeed.

MOM

I wrote this poem for my mom because she and I could never get along, and when the Lord Jesus Christ saved me, our relationship only became worse. She loved this poem and read it every day while she was able.

For all those years I wouldn't listen and just would not obey.

I thank God for his loving hand that sought my soul that summer's day.

He said, "Son, it's time to listen. I want you for my own. I'll teach you the right path to take, the one that will get you home!"

Mom, I know it hasn't been easy for you to understand, but I thank you for being my mommy no matter where I am.

So as time passes on and on, remember this is true. Just keep on trusting Jesus, and forever I'll be with you!

Chris

SOULS AT DEL TACO

While I was still living in El Cajon, California, I had a welding business that allowed me to work at whatever time I chose to. At lunch time I would go to Del Taco to eat, and when I was finished, I would start to preach the Word of God. So there I was being used by Jesus to tell people that they must be born again to get into heaven (John 3:3–8). I would preach for about two hours a day Monday through Friday, and I did that for two months. I would ask God to let somebody hear me and get saved.

So about sixteen years later, my wife Carmen and I were going over to visit my mom and stopped at that same Del Taco for lunch. As we were looking at the menu, I noticed a woman preparing the food orders, and I leaned over and asked Carmen, "See that woman? She was working here sixteen years ago, back when I used to preach here!"

So I asked the woman if she remembered me, and she said, "Yes, I do, and I used to listen to you preach while I worked!"

Then she said to me, "And guess what? My family and I all got born again. We're all saved!"

Well, I don't have words to describe how I felt when she said that, but I do know what the Bible says about it. It says that every angel in heaven rejoices over one sinner that repents (Luke 15:10). And yes, I thanked the Lord for hearing my prayer and saving them.

Please remember, Jesus said: "You must be born again to get into Heaven (John 3:3–8)". Ask Jesus to save you. Do it today!

Lightning Source UK Ltd.
Milton Keynes UK
UKHW011010080320
359928UK00002B/31/J

9 781796 090109